NOTE TO PARENTS

Welcome to Kingfisher Readers! This program is designed to help young readers build skills, confidence, and a love of reading as they explore their favorite topics.

These tips can help you get more from the experience of reading books together. But remember, the most important thing is to make reading fun!

Tips to Warm Up Before Reading

- Look through the book with your child. Ask them what they notice about the pictures.
- Wonder aloud together. Ask questions and make predictions. What will this book be about? What are some words we could expect to find on these pages?

While Reading

- Take turns or read together until your child takes over.
- Point to the words as you say them.
- When your child gets stuck on a word, ask if the picture could help. Then think about the first letter too.
- Accept and praise your child's contributions.

After Reading

- Look back at the things your child found interesting. Encourage connections to other things you both know.
- Draw pictures or make models to explore these ideas.
- Read the book again soon, to build fluency.

With five distinct levels and a wealth of appealing topics, the Kingfisher Readers series provides children with an exciting way to learn to read and wonder about the world around them. Enjoy!

Ellie Costa, M.S. Ed.
Literacy Specialist, Bank Street School for Children, New York

KINGFISHER
READERS

level
1

Jobs
People Do

Thea Feldman

KINGFISHER
NEW YORK

KINGFISHER
LONDON & NEW YORK

Copyright © Kingfisher 2012
Published in the United States by Kingfisher,
175 Fifth Ave., New York, NY 10010
Kingfisher is an imprint of Macmillan Children's Books, London.
All rights reserved.

Distributed in the U.S. and Canada by Macmillan,
175 Fifth Ave., New York, NY 10010

Library of Congress Cataloging-in-Publication data
has been applied for.

Series editor: Thea Feldman
Literacy consultant: Ellie Costa, Bank St. College, New York

ISBN: 978-0-7534-6847-0 (HB)
ISBN: 978-0-7534-6845-6 (PB)

Kingfisher books are available for special promotions
and premiums. For details contact: Special Markets
Department, Macmillan, 175 Fifth Ave.,
New York, NY 10010.

For more information, please visit
www.kingfisherbooks.com

Printed in China
9 8 7 6 5 4 3 2 1
1TR/1011/WKT/UNTD/105MA

Picture credits
The Publisher would like to thank the following for permission to reproduce their material.
Every care has been taken to trace copyright holders. However, if there have been unintentional
omissions or failure to trace copyright holders, we apologize and will, if informed, endeavor
to make corrections in any future edition.
Top = t; Bottom = b; Center = c; Left = l; Right = r
Cover Photolibrary/Index Stock imagery; Pages 3cl Corbis/Edward Bock; 3cr Shutterstock/Monkey Business
Images; 3bl Corbis/Angel Wynn/Nativestock; 3br Corbis/Kelly-Mooney Photography; 4 Shutterstock/iofoto;
5 Corbis/LWA-Dann Tardif; 6 Shutterstock/Stephen Coburn; 7 Photolibrary/White; 8 Photolibrary/White;
9 Corbis/Richard T. Nowitz; 10 Shutterstock/CandyBoxPhoto; 11 Photolibrary/White; 12 Corbis/Patrick Lane/
Somos Images; 13 Corbis/Ariel Skelley/Blend Images; 14 Shutterstock/OtnaYdur; 15 Corbis/Anderson Ross/
Blend Images; 16 Alamy/Blend Images; 17 Alamy/fStop; 18 Alamy/Steve Skjold; 19 Photolibrary/Cuboimages;
20 Shutterstock/Lars Christiansen; 20b Corbis/Marc Mueller/dpa; 21 Photolibrary/Bios; 22–23 Getty/NASA;
24 Photolibrary/ Index Stock Imagery; 25 Photolibrary/ Index Stock Imagery; 26 Getty/Michael Steele;
27 Photolibrary/Imagebroker; 28 Shutterstock/Lurii Osadchi; 29 Shutterstock/Igor Bulgarin;
30tr Corbis/Paul Burns; 30cl Alamy/Blend Images; 30b Shutterstock/Kurhan;
31c Shutterstock/pistolseven; 31b Shutterstock/Denis Sabo.

It is a busy day!

People are working.

They are doing their jobs.

What are some jobs people do?

There are many jobs
in your town.

A **teacher** does one job
you know.

A teacher helps kids
learn many things.

4

You know the job a **mail carrier** does too.

A mail carrier brings the mail to your home.

This person helps build new homes.

These people help
other people move.

Police officers work
to keep your town safe.

Firefighters put out fires.

They keep the town safe too.

A **doctor** in your town helps sick people feel better.

This doctor helps
sick animals
feel better!

She is called a **vet**.

There are many jobs in the stores in town too.

A **grocer** sells food for your family to eat at home.

Someone adds up the prices
so your family can pay.

Someone puts the food in bags.

Do you like to eat
in a restaurant?

The cook
is called
a **chef**.

What is this
chef making?

Someone brings
your food.

Yum!

Whose shop do you visit
when you need a haircut?

The hair-cutter's shop!

At the flower
shop, someone
sells flowers
and plants.

A bus driver works in town.

A taxi driver may work
in town too.

A taxi driver takes
people where they
need to go.

A **pilot** flies an airplane.

A pilot's job takes him
far from home.

There are more jobs
that happen far from home.

This person studies animals
where the animals live!

An **astronaut** works in space to help us learn about it.

An astronaut's job is *really* far from home!

A farmer's job is where he lives.

He lives in a house on a farm.

A farmer may plant food,
such as corn.

He may have cows
and chickens.

Some jobs may not look like work.

But they are!

Soccer players work hard to win a game.

Goal!

A zookeeper feeds the animals at the zoo.

People in a band play music.

They work hard to sound good!

A dancer does her job
on a stage.

There are so many jobs
people do.

What do you want to do
when you grow up?

Is it in this book?

Glossary

astronaut someone who works in space

chef someone who cooks in a restaurant

doctor someone who helps sick people get well

firefighters people who put out fires

grocer someone who works in a grocery store

mail carrier someone who delivers the mail

pilot someone who flies an airplane

police officers people who keep your neighborhood safe

teacher someone who helps you learn many things

vet a doctor who helps animals feel better

If you have enjoyed reading this book, look out for more in the Kingfisher Readers series!

KINGFISHER READERS: LEVEL 1

Baby Animals
Butterflies
Colorful Coral Reefs
Jobs People Do
Snakes Alive!
Trains

KINGFISHER READERS: LEVEL 2

What Animals Eat
Your Body

KINGFISHER READERS: LEVEL 3

Dinosaur World
Volcanoes

KINGFISHER READERS: LEVEL 4

Pirates
Weather

KINGFISHER READERS: LEVEL 5

Ancient Egyptians
Rainforests

For a full list of Kingfisher Readers books, plus guidance for teachers and parents and activities and fun stuff for kids, go to the Kingfisher Readers website: www.kingfisherreaders.com